FERRIES
of the
IRISH SEA
Past and Present

Brittany Ferries

DUCHESSE ANNE

Published by

FERRY
Publications Ltd

ISBN: 1 871947 45 6

PO Box 9, Narberth, Pembrokeshire, SA68 0YT. Tel: +44 (0) 1834 891460 Fax: +44 (0) 1834 891463

Since the entry into the EU of Britain and Ireland, the passenger and freight services on the Irish Sea have expanded at a rapid rate. Prior to this, the operations had been very traditional with few companies rivalling those of Sealink, B & I and Townsend Thoresen, who held the monopoly of operations between the UK and Ireland. It was not until 1968 that a ferry service was opened linking Ireland and France. Compared to the ferry operations on the English Channel of the day, the ships and the port installations lacked modernisation and major investment. It was not until 1965 that a drive-on/drive-off ferry service opened between Holyhead and Dun Laoghaire using the *Holyhead Ferry I*, and it was not until some seven years' later that a similar operation was opened at Fishguard. This type of operation had been established at Dover since 1952 and at Southampton in 1964. By the early seventies, the two state-controlled ferry companies, Sealink and B & I, controlled the passenger services between the UK and the Republic of Ireland with a fleet of fairly old tonnage. Increased competition from the airlines was also to see a gradual rationalisation of services on the Irish Sea during the late seventies, and there have been major changes to all passenger operations. There has been a major expansion of trade in the freight market in the last ten years, and indicators point to continued growth in this sector with the economy of Ireland continuing to grow into the next century.

Today, the Irish Sea has a wide variety of vessels, not all of which are suitable for the rigours of the Irish Sea. The formerly nationalised firms of Sealink and B & I have been privatised, being replaced by Stena Line and Irish Ferries, both of which continue to rival each other. In the light of this competition, Irish Ferries have recently introduced two purpose-built vessels on their routes from Dublin and Rosslare.

Title Page: Brittany Ferries' *Duchesse Anne* was originally built for B & I to open their Cork-Pembroke Dock service in 1979. Following financial problems with B & I, the vessel was subsequently sold to Brittany Ferries. *(FotoFlite)*

Above: B & I Line opened a rival ferry service to that of the established Fishguard-Rosslare route in 1979 from Rosslare to Pembroke Dock. One of the many vessels that operated prior to 1997 was the *Innisfallen*. She is seen here leaving Pembroke Dock for Rosslare. *(Miles Cowsill)*

Possibly one of the most famous ships to operate on the Irish Sea in the last 20 years is Sealink's *St. Columba*. She is seen here arriving at Holyhead from Dun Laoghaire. The Folkestone-based *Vortigern* can be seen in the dry-dock at the port undergoing an overhaul. *(Ferry Publications Library)*

Meanwhile, Stena Line initially introduced a fast ferry service between Holyhead and Dun Laoghaire in 1993, which was followed quickly by a similar service between Fishguard and Rosslare. Today, the Holyhead route, with the Stranraer-Belfast service, have two revolutionary HSS craft, both of which have brought a completely new style of travel for passengers between the UK and Ireland.

In 1984, B & I closed their Cork-Pembroke Dock service, claiming that they could no longer sustain this loss-making route. Some three years' later, three local authorities in Ireland, Cork Corporation, Cork County Council and Kerry County Council, together with West Glamorgan County Council and Swansea City Council, co-operated to form a new company, Swansea Cork Ferries. They subsequently introduced the *Celtic Pride* on the new nine hour route from Cork to Swansea. The Polish-registered vessel remained on the link for the next two years, no service materialised in 1989 but resumed again in 1990 with the Greek-owned ferry the *Ioniah Sun* (ex. *Leinster*) maintaining the link. The *Celtic Pride* returned again in 1991 until she was replaced two years later by another Greek ship the *Superferry,* at which time the company was acquired by the Greek company Strintzis Lines. The *Superferry* has maintained the nine-hour link since, the company hope to replace her in the near future.

The new Rosslare-Pembroke Dock route was opened by B & I in 1981 with the chartered Townsend Thoresen vessel *Viking III*. She was followed by a series of unsuitable vessels on the link until 1997, when the eminently suitable *Isle of Innisfree* from Holyhead was transferred to the Southern Corridor. This new multi-purpose vessel with well-appointed accommodation, extensive vehicle decks and reliability during inclement weather has proved an immediate success for the route.

The introduction of the *Stena Normandica* in 1979, later renamed *St Brendan*, by Sealink was a dramatic change for the long-established Fishguard-Rosslare service. The Swedish vessel maintained the link until 1990 when she was replaced by the *Felicity*, later renamed *Stena Felicity*. The 'Felicity' set a new standard of service on the route from that of the *Stena Normandica* and was to play a vital role in the expansion of the service over the next seven years in tandem with the new fast ferry operation of the *Stena Lynx*, introduced in 1994. In 1997 the *Stena Felicity's* career on the Southern Corridor came to an end when she was required by her owners back in the Baltic for the next season. She was replaced by the *Koningin Beatrix* from the Harwich-Hook service, the former Dutch-registered vessel, whilst again setting higher standards of passenger facilities has not proved an overriding success on the route during bad weather.

The Continental services of Irish Ferries have had mixed fortunes with *Saint Killian II* and *Saint Patrick II*. With the major investment in their UK-Ireland operations in the last couple of years, Irish Ferries addressed their Continental operations in 1998 with the replacement of the two older ships by the chartered *Normandy* (ex. *St Nicholas*, ex. *Stena Normandy*). At the same time the company also decided to concentrate on only one ferry port in Ireland, Rosslare, and to close their Le Havre operations in favour of concentrating their services on Cherbourg and Roscoff.

Brittany Ferries opened their Continental operation between France and Ireland in 1978 with the *Armorique*. Their operations have been blessed with good fortunes, in spite of the demise of the more recent St. Malo-Cork service. The once-weekly service between Roscoff and Cork is currently maintained by the luxuriously-appointed *Val de Loire* and *Quiberon*. The Port of Cork has seen other ferry services during the last twenty years, one of the most recent operations is that of Gaelic Ferries who initially chartered the *Purbeck* to open their freight link to Cherbourg. Their operations are currently suspended pending availability of a suitable vessel.

The Holyhead-Dun Laoghaire route has changed beyond all recognition since the introduction of Stena Line's HSS service in 1996. Sadly, this long-established route has seen the demise of a traditional passenger ferry since the introduction of the *Stena Explorer*. Not all passengers have welcomed the introduction of the HSS and their rivals operating to Dublin, Irish Ferries, have seen a dramatic growth on their route in the last two years with one of northern Europe's largest ferries, the *Isle of Inishmore*. In 1999 Irish Ferries plan to introduce their own fast ferry service.

The continued growth in Ireland and a major capital investment in the City of Dublin, has seen the re-establishment of the Liverpool-Dublin route following the demise of B&I's service in 1987 and Sealink's in 1990. Last year, Sea Containers introduced the Isle of Man Steam Packet vessel *Lady of Mann* on the route, her success was followed by a new fast ferry service with the *SuperSeaCat Two* this year. Another rival ferry operation is due to start in early 1999 with Merchant Ferries, who plan not only to carry their traditional freight customers but also to introduce a passenger service to Dublin.

Following the demise of Belfast Ferries' route between Liverpool and Belfast in 1991, Norse Irish Ferries have gradually turned the route's fortunes around. Two new purpose-built ferries have entered service during the last twelve months and today they offer departures each night and a thrice weekly daylight operation.

One of the longest-established ferry services on the Irish Sea is that of the Isle of Man Steam Packet Company. The decline of the holiday traffic to the Island has sadly seen their fleet drop to only three vessels in 1998. Further radical changes were made to the company this year, with the withdrawal of the passenger ship *King Orry* and freight vessel *Peveril*. Both vessels were replaced by a multi-purpose Ro-Pax ship by the name of *Ben my Chree* in August 1998. The future of the *Lady of Mann* is uncertain, the long-term service to the Island will be operated by the multi-purpose vessel *Ben-my-Chree* and a fast craft - a sad demise in the fortunes in the holiday trade to the Isle of Man from that of the post-war years.

The Port of Heysham, owned by Sea Containers, has seen enormous growth in freight traffic

Above: The *Ionic Ferry* pictured at Preston during her first season in service on the Northern Ireland link in 1958. *(Ferry Publications Library)*

Below: A late evening scene at Fleetwood with the *Mona's Queen* seen arriving at the port from Douglas. *(Ferry Publications Library)*

The *Europic Ferry* was built for the Atlantic Steam Navigation Company in 1967. She transferred to the Irish Sea in 1983, principally a freight ship on the Larne-Cairnryan service. In her final year of service, she was renamed *European Freighter* by P&O European Ferries. *(Ferry Publications Library)*

during the last ten years. Currently four operators use the port, the Isle of Man Steam Packet Company, with both their passenger and freight operations, Merchant Ferries, Belfast Freight Ferries (who have recently been taken over by Merchant Ferries parent company, Cenargo) and Seatruck Ferries.

At Stranraer, the route has seen the introduction of a fast ferry link using the second of the purpose-built HSS craft, the *Stena Voyager*. The Stranraer route is no longer linked with Larne but with Belfast. This initially was to see a dramatic decrease in passenger levels for Stena Line but recently fortunes have changed. The rival service of SeaCat Scotland from Stranraer to Belfast has continued to see good growth since it was established in 1990 using *SeaCat Scotland*.

P&O European Ferries' operations at Cairnryan have recently been newly merged with those of Pandoro who have operated links on the Irish Sea between Rosslare-Cherbourg, Liverpool-Dublin, Fleetwood-Larne and Ardrossan-Larne. The newly-merged company, P&O European Ferries (Irish Sea), have eleven vessels on the Irish Sea, all of which will need replacement in the next ten years. Three of their vessels, the *European Envoy* (ex. *Ibex*), the *European Leader* (ex. *Buffalo*) and the *European Pioneer* (ex. *Bison*) have been jumboised in recent years to offer greater capacity and meet increasingly stringent safety requirements. Alongside the freight operations of this company is the fast ferry service of the *Jetliner*, which can cross between Ireland and Scotland in just one hour.

There may be a slight over-capacity of vessels currently on the Irish Sea but with the continued growth of trade between Ireland's EU neighbours, Britain and France, the fortunes of the present ferry operators should continue. The ending of Duty Free may however see a further reduction in the choice and quality of services on offer to passenger and freight customers and may result in higher charges. The resulting uncertainty is detrimental to investment in the current and future ferry services.

This publication includes a wide variety of pictures of some of the many vessels that have operated on the Irish Sea during the last twenty years, many of which still operate today. I am indebted to my business partner, John Hendy, for his guidance with the book and to Gordon Hislip, Jack Phelan and Matthew Punter for their assistance with the book.

Miles Cowsill

The *Saint Killian II* seen on passage to Rosslare from Le Havre. *(Ferry Publications Library)*

Above: The **Celtic Pride** seen at Ringaskiddy Terminal, Cork pending her morning departure to Swansea. Swansea Cork Ferries was established in 1987 to re-open the Swansea-Cork service abandoned by B & I Line in 1979. *(Gordon Hislip)*

Below: This view of Ringaskiddy, Cork shows the Greek-registered **Ionian Sun** (ex. B & I vessel **Leinster**). She was chartered from Strintzis Line in 1990 to maintain the service in the absence of the **Celtic Pride** which was not available for the route. *(Gordon Hislip)*

Above: The Japanese-built *Superferry* approaches Swansea harbour in 1996 from Cork. In 1991, she was sold to Strintzis Line and was briefly renamed ***Ionian Express***. Following major rebuilding, she was renamed the ***Superferry*** and used on their services in Greece. Since 1993 she has been used on the Swansea Cork Ferries' route. *(Matthew Punter)*

Below: Following the reduction of Irish Ferries' services to the Continent in 1997, Gaelic Ferries established their own operation from Cork to Cherbourg using the ***Purbeck***. The former Truckline vessel is seen here arriving from Cherbourg with the town of Cobh behind her. In April,1998 the ***Purbeck*** returned to the English Channel and Gaelic Ferries then chartered the ***Francoise*** to maintain their operations. The company hope in the future to find a suitable ro-pax vessel for their services. *(Jack Phelan)*

Above: The **Stena Challenger** is seen here arriving at Cork whilst on charter to convey the Tour de France Championship party to Roscoff in July 1998. *(Jack Phelan)*

Below: The French registered **Quiberon** seen at Ringaskiddy Terminal in April 1990 pending her afternoon departure to Roscoff. *(Gordon Hislip)*

Above: Brittany Ferries' *Bretagne* is seen here arriving at Cork from Roscoff in May 1991. She was built originally for the Plymouth-Santander and Roscoff-Cork routes, and today she operates between Portsmouth and St. Malo. *(Miles Cowsill)*

Below: The much-travelled *Armorique* is seen here arriving at Rosslare from Le Havre whilst on charter to Irish Ferries in March 1993. Some fifteen years earlier she had opened the passenger service of Brittany Ferries between Roscoff and Cork in 1978. *(Gordon Hislip)*

The *Saint Patrick II* seen at Rosslare following her arrival from Le Havre in July 1996. Originally built as the *Aurella* for service in the Baltic, she was purchased by Irish Ferries in 1982 to maintain their Continental links in the summer. With no winter work for her during a number of seasons she was chartered out to various companies, including North Sea Ferries, P&O European Ferries and Stena Line. The view below shows the *Saint Patrick II* en-route back from the Baltic after her charter to Tallink. *(Miles Cowsill/FotoFlite)*

Right: The *Saint Killian II* seen arriving at Rosslare from Le Havre during her last season in July 1997. Following completing her season on the Continental services of Irish Ferries, she was sent to lay-up and sale with her former operating partner, the *Saint Patrick II*. *(Miles Cowsill)*

Below: Irish Ferries chartered the former Sealink vessel *Stena Normandy* in 1998 to maintain their Continental services, as neither the *Saint Patrick II* nor the *Saint Killian II* met the required SOLAS standards. The *Normandy* is seen here arriving at Pembroke Dock whilst covering for the *Isle of Innisfree* on her refit in March 1998. *(Miles Cowsill)*

Above: The *Viking III* opened the Rosslare-Pembroke Dock service in May 1980. The Townsend-Thoresen vessel is seen here at Rosslare at the newly-constructed B & I berth in August 1980. *(Miles Cowsill)*.

Below: This interesting view shows the *Innisfallen* inward from Cork with the German built *Munster* outward-bound to Rosslare. *(Ferry Publications Library)*

Above: This interesting view shows the *Innisfallen* leaving Pembroke Dock in June 1984 for her four hour journey to Rosslare. *(Miles Cowsill)*

Below: The *Connacht* was originally built for the Cork-Pembroke Dock service, however with continued losses within the group, she was transferred later to operate on the Dublin-Liverpool service with her near-sister, the *Leinster*. The *Connacht* is seen outward-bound here in the Liffey sporting the then new livery of the company. *(Ferry Publications Library)*

Above: The former Sealink vessel *Earl Harold* is seen here leaving Pembroke Dock whilst on charter to B & I Line on the Rosslare-Pembroke Dock route in 1989. She was one of a series of charters on the route which were totally unsuitable. *(Miles Cowsill)*

Below: The *Isle of Inishmore* (ex *Leinster*) seen arriving at Rosslare in July 1994, She was sold in 1997 to Canadian interests. *(Gordon Hislip)*

Above: This interesting view shows the chartered *Isle of Innisfree* (ex *Niels Klim*) at the linkspan at Pembroke Dock with Hoverspeed's SeaCat *Hoverspeed Boulogne* (now *SeaCat Danmark*) arriving for refuelling from Folkestone en-route to Stranraer. *(Miles Cowsill)*

Below: The *Isle of Innisfree* is pictured here prior to her launch at the yard of Van der Giessen, Holland. The *Isle of Innisfree* was initially placed on the Dublin-Holyhead route. On the delivery of her near-sister the *Isle of Inishmore*, she was then transferred to the Rosslare-Pembroke Dock route. *(Ferry Publications Library)*

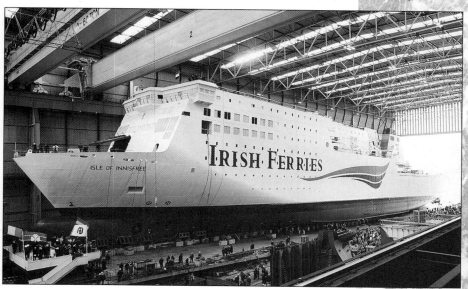

Above: In 1979 Sealink introduced the chartered *Stena Normandica* from Sweden. The vessel is seen here arriving at Rosslare during her first season on the Fishguard route. *(Miles Cowsill)*
Below: The *St Brendan* (**ex *Stena Normandica***) was replaced by the ***Stena Felicity*** in 1990. The Swedish-registered vessel is seen here at Rosslare in July 1994 sporting the livery of Stena Sealink Line. *(Gordon Hislip)*

Above: The *Stena Felicity* is captured here arriving in the evening sun at Rosslare in May 1996. *(Gordon Hislip)*

Below: This unusual view shows *Condor 10* at Rosslare whilst on charter to Stena Line in place of the *Stena Lynx* which was unavailable for the route in 1996. This craft was originally built for the Channel Island operations. *(Gordon Hislip)*

Prior to the departure of the **Stena Felicity** in June 1997, the Irish Sea experienced some very inclement weather. As a result, the **Stena Felicity** was forced to use the more protected harbour of Pembroke Dock. She is seen here above, arriving at the Pembrokeshire port during her last few days in service. *(Miles Cowsill)*

The view to the left shows the **Koningin Beatrix** leaving Pembroke Dock during the same period, whilst supporting the **Stena Felicity** prior to her departure.
(Miles Cowsill)

Above: The *Koningin Beatrix* is seen in this view arriving from Holland on berthing trials at Rosslare on 22nd June 1997. She was displaced from the Harwich-Hook service on the entry into service of the HSS *Stena Discovery*. *(Miles Cowsill)*

Below: The *Stena Lynx* seen arriving at Rosslare in July 1997, following her 99 minute crossing from Fishguard. It seems likely that she will be replaced with a larger craft in 1999. *(Miles Cowsill)*

Above: The *Cambridge Ferry* was transferred from Dover to the Irish Sea prior to the entry into service of the *Nord Pas de Calais* in 1987. She was utilised principally at Fishguard, until the entry of the *Stena Felicity*, when she was displaced. She is seen here arriving at Fishguard for the first time. *(Miles Cowsill)*
Below: The *Hengist* was used on the Fishguard-Rosslare route for a short spell in 1985. The Folkestone based vessel is seen outward bound from Fishguard. *(Miles Cowsill)*

Above: This interesting view shows the **Stena Caledonia** at Rosslare dressed overall whilst on charter to the 'Tour de France' in July 1998. *(Philip Booth)*

Below: The **Stena Londoner** seen arriving at Fishguard whilst covering for the refit of the **Stena Felicity**. After a short spell at Fishguard and Holyhead, she was transferred back to her owners SeaFrance. Today the ship is named the **SeaFrance Monet** and is the reserve ship on the Dover-Calais route for Sea France. *(Miles Cowsill)*

Above & Below: Pandoro established a freight-only service between Rosslare and Cherbourg in 1993 with the former Dover-based vessel *European Clearway*. The top view is of the vessel departing from Rosslare in 1998, renamed the *European Pathfinder*. The view below shows her near-sister the *European Endeavour* arriving from Dublin on a rare visit to Rosslare whilst on the Cherbourg-Rosslare route in July 1997. *(Gordon Hislip/Miles Cowsill)*

Above: An unusual view of the *Koningin Beatrix* seen passing Cobh inward from Rosslare pending her charter to the Tour de France in 1998. *(Jack Phelan)*
Below: The *Quiberon* seen leaving Ringaskiddy Terminal for Roscoff in June 1995. The vessel maintains the Roscoff-Plymouth service today and operates to Ireland out of season in place of of the *Val de Loire*. *(Miles Cowsill)*

Two old faithful vessels of the Irish Sea. The top shows the the **Isle of Inishmore** leaving Pembroke Dock for Rosslare in 1995. The view below takes in the **Saint Patrick II** leaving Rosslare during her last season in service. *(Miles Cowsill)*

Top: The *St David* was originally built for the Fishguard-Rosslare route in 1981, in the event she was used on the Holyhead route to boost freight traffic on the link. She is seen here at Fishguard whilst covering for the *Stena Normandica* in 1983. *(Miles Cowsill)*
Below: The *Stena Normandica* seen leaving Fishguard in the new livery of Sealink in 1984. *(Miles Cowsill)*

arl William pictured at Milford Haven after the end of Liverpool-Dun Laoghaire service in 1990. (*Miles Cowsill*)

The **King Orry** seen at the Victoria Pier, Douglas during her mid-week lay-up in August 1998.
(Miles Cowsill)

Above: The *Ben-my-Chree* seen arriving at Douglas on her first daylight sailing with the company on 4th August 1998. The *King Orry* can be seen laid-up behind her for peak weekend sailings. *(Miles Cowsill)*
Below: The *SuperSeaCat Two* seen arriving at Dublin during her first season on the Liverpool-Dublin route. The vessel can cross between both ports in under four hours. *(Gordon Hislip)*

Above: The *European Seafarer* (ex *Puma*) seen arriving at Dublin from Liverpool on 1st May 1998. *(Gordon Hislip)*
Below: A dull Spring day in this view shows the *Europic Ferry* outward bound from Scotland to Larne. The 'Europic' was the last ASN vessel to be built for the company before its takeover by Townsend Thoresen. *(Miles Cowsill)*

The **St. Columba** was delivered to Sealink in 1977 to maintain the Holyhead-Dun Laoghaire route. She operated on the link until 1996, as the principal ferry on the route. The top view shows her as originally built as the **St. Columba** leaving Dun Laoghaire for Anglesey. The view below shows her arriving at Dun Laoghaire following an extensive overhaul and having been renamed **Stena Hibernia**. *(Gordon Hislip)*

Above: The former Folkestone-based *Horsa* was transferred from the English Channel to the Holyhead-Dun Laoghaire route in 1990 to offer additional capacity on the route. She is seen here leaving Dun Laoghaire for Wales. *(Miles Cowsill)*

Below: With increased freight capacity required on the Holyhead-Dun Laoghaire route, the *Stena Cambria* (ex *St. Anselm*) was transferred to the Irish Sea. The former Folkestone-based vessel is seen here arriving at Holyhead during her last season in 1995. *(Miles Cowsill)*

Above: The **Stena Adventurer** (ex **St. Columba,** ex **Stena Hibernia**) is pictured here at the Salt Island berth during her last season on the route in Stena Line livery following the demise of the Sealink brand name by the Swedish company. *(Miles Cowsill)*

Below: A late evening view of the **Stena Antrim** leaving Dun Laoghaire in January 1995 for Holyhead whilst covering for the refits on the route. *(Gordon Hislip)*

Above: In 1993 Stena Sealink Line introduced a fast ferry service between Holyhead and Dun Laoghaire. The first vessel to open this new operation was the InCat craft *Stena Sea Lynx*. She is seen here loading at Rosslare for Fishguard in 1994. *(Miles Cowsill)*

Below: The *Stena Sea Lynx II* replaced the smaller InCat craft in 1994, which allowed her to be displaced to the Fishguard-Rosslare route. The larger craft is seen here alongside at Dun Laoghaire. *(Gordon Hislip)*

Left: The Holyhead-Dun Laoghaire route has seen a variety of vessels covering during the refit periods in the winter. One of the regular visitors to the Irish Sea has been the **Norrona** pictured here arriving at Dun Laoghaire in February 1994. *(Gordon Hislip)*

Below: Sealink British Ferries announced plans in 1987 that they would start an all-year-round service between Liverpool and Dun Laoghaire, using the **Earl William**. Due to mechanical problems in her first season and the company's failure to introduce a second ship , the route closed some 20 months' later. The **Earl William** is seen here arriving at Liverpool for the last time. *(Ferry Publications Library)*

Stena Line opened a new freight service between Dublin and Holyhead in 1995 with the **Stena Traveller**. The chartered vessel was subsequently replaced by her near-sister, the **Stena Challenger** (pictured below) in September 1996. *(Gordon Hislip/Miles Cowsill)*

Economics eventually forced B & I Line to close their Dublin-Liverpool route in favour of the shorter crossing between Holyhead and Dublin. The top view shows the *Isle of Inishmore* leaving Dublin in April 1993 for Holyhead. In 1995, following the demise of B & I Line, Irish Ferries introduced a multi-purpose vessel for the route by the name of the *Isle of Innisfree*. The 'Innisfree' is seen below at Holyhead. *(Gordon Hislip)*

The top view shows the *Isle of Inishmore* shortly after her launch from the yard of Van der Giessen in Holland. The *Isle of Inishmore* replaced the *Isle of Innisfree* on the Dublin route in 1997. The picture below shows the new vessel shortly after her arrival from the builders. *(Ferry Publications Library/Gordon Hislip)*

Above: The *Isle of Innisfree* seen outward-bound from Dublin during her last season on the route prior to her transfer to the Southern Corridor. *(Gordon Hislip)*

Below: This interesting view shows the chartered *Munster* and the *Saint Killian II* at the North Wall extension at Dublin in March 1993. The *Munster* had recently completed her charter to B & I on the Rosslare-Pembroke Dock route. *(Gordon Hislip)*

Above: Such was the growth of freight in 1996 that Irish Ferries chartered the **Purbeck** from Channel Island Ferries. The vessel is seen here arriving in Dublin sporting the Sally logo on her side. *(Gordon Hislip)*

Below: The **Lady of Mann** awaits the Irish Ferries berth at Dublin, as the **Isle of Inishmore** gets underway for Holyhead. *(Gordon Hislip)*

Above: In 1998, Sea Containers replaced the *Lady of Mann* with the fast craft *SuperSeaCat Two.* This view shows her arriving at Dublin during her first few weeks in operation from Liverpool . *(Gordon Hislip)*

Below: The *Lady of Mann* has been a regular visitor to the port of Dublin during her distinguished career on the Irish Sea. In 1997 she opened a regular ferry service between Liverpool and Dublin. She is seen here arriving at Dublin having just taken onboard the pilot. *(Gordon Hislip)*

Pandoro for many years have had a strong grip on the Irish Sea freight services. The top view takes in the **Puma** departing from Dublin Port bound for Liverpool in March 1995. The vessel's near-sister and operating partner, the **Leopard** (ex **Viking Trader**), is seen below leaving the linkspan at Dublin. *(Gordon Hislip)*

Above: Jumboisation work certainly did not improve the looks of the *Ibex,* subsequently renamed *European Envoy*. This view shows the additional upper freight deck following the ship undergoing conversion work at Cammell Laird. The view to the right shows the ship as the *Norsky* prior to her conversion and renaming. *(Timothy Cowsill/Gordon Hislip)*

Both the **Bison** and **Buffalo** have recently received additional freight capacity following jumboisation work. The top view takes in the **Buffalo** leaving Dublin prior to this work and the picture below shows the **Bison** following conversion work leaving Ireland for Liverpool in February 1997. *(Gordon Hislip)*

Above: This view shows the *European Leader* (ex *Buffalo*) following her conversion works in 1998. She still retains very much her orginal profile following her jumboisation in stark contrast to her near sister - see page 46. **Left:** Pandoro have chartered many vessels to maintain their operations on the Irish Sea over the last 10 years. Pictured left is the former Channel Islands' vessel *Commodore Clipper* arriving at Dublin in May 1996. Below: This shows the *Tidero Star* leaving the same year for Liverpool. *(All photos Gordon Hislip)*

In 1997, following the demise of the Eurolink service between Sheerness and Vlissingen, the **Euromantique** was chartered by Pandoro. The Greek ship is seen here at night pending her evening departure to Liverpool. The view below takes in the chartered **Seahawk**, again seen at P&O Pandoro Terminal at Dublin. *(Gordon Hislip)*

Above: Merchant Ferries have continued to see major freight growth on the Irish Sea in recent years. Today they operate between Heysham and Liverpool (as from 1999) to Dublin. Two of their vessels are seen here, the top view shows the *Merchant Brilliant* outward-bound to Heysham and the view below shows the smaller of their units, the *Moondance*, laid up at Dublin prior to taking up service with Seatruck. The vessel is no longer in the fleet of the company. *(Gordon Hislip)*

Above: Built originally for the Dunkerque - Dover train ferry service as the **Saint Eloi**, the **King Orry** has been valuable tonnage for the Isle of Man Steam Packet Co. since she was introduced in 1991. She is seen here arriving at Douglas in an all-white livery in August 1997, which was changed in 1998 for a blue hull - see page 30. *(Miles Cowsill)*

Below: This view shows the **Ben-my-Chree** en-route to Isle of Man from her builders in Holland. She has very similar looks to that of both the **Isle of Innisfree** and **Isle of Inishmore**, but of course is much smaller to be able to fit Douglas Harbour *(FotoFlite)*

Right The *Peveril* has maintained a vital freight link between the UK and the Isle of Man since 1981. She was withdrawn from service in July 1998 on the arrival of the *Ben-my-Chree* *(Ferry Publications Library)*

Below: The *SeaCat Danmark* replaced the *SeaCat Isle of Man* in 1998. The former *Hoverspeed Boulogne* is seen here leaving Douglas for Belfast in July 1998. *(Miles Cowsill)*

Above: Following Merchant Ferries' decision to concentrate their services on Dublin instead of Warrenpoint, Seatruck Ferries established their own operation between Heysham and Warrenpoint. The first of their vessels, the chartered **Bolero**, is seen here at Heysham. *(Miles Cowsill)*

Below: Following Stena Line's decision to withdraw from Larne in favour of Belfast in 1996, they later established a fast ferry service using the HSS craft **Stena Voyager**. The **Stena Voyager** and the **Stena Caledonia** are pictured here at Belfast. *(Miles Cowsill)*

Above: Belfast Freight Ferries currently operate four vessels on their service between Heysham and Belfast. One of these is the **Saga Moon**, seen here leaving Heysham with the **King Orry** in the background. *(Matthew Punter)*

Below: Following the demise of P&O Ferries' service between Liverpool and Belfast, Belfast Ferries re-established the route using the **St. Colum I** (ex. **Saint Patrick**). Whilst the vessel offered adequate accommodation for her passengers she lacked the freight capacity which eventually was to see the demise of the service. *(Ferry Publications Library)*

Above: Norse Irish Ferries once again re-established the Liverpool-Belfast service with a series of chartered vessels. In 1997 they introduced the first of two purpose built ships on the route, the ***Mersey Viking*** which was built in Italy. The ***Norse Mersey*** can be seen at the berth prior to being withdrawn from service *(Norse Irish Ferries)*

Below: The ***Darnia*** pictured from the bridge of the ***Europic Ferry***. She played a vital role for Sealink on their freight operations on the North Channel until 1991 when she was sold by the company for further service on the Baltic. *(Miles Cowsill)*

Above: The last surviving 'Free Enterprise' class vessel in the UK, the **Pride of Rathlin** in 1998, is seen here leaving Larne. The looks of this vessel were not improved by her jumboisation in 1986, however she has been an extremely valuable vessel to the fleet for over 25 years. *(Miles Cowsill)*

Below: *The **SeaCat Scotland** at Belfast during her first season on the fast ferry route on the north channel. She is due to be replaced by a SuperSeaCat in 2000. (Ferry Publications Library)*

Above: This view shows Pandoro's freight vessel *Lion* arriving at Dublin on a special sailing away from her usual Ardrossan-Larne duties in 1997. She has subsequently been renamed ***European Highlander*** *(Gordon Hislip)*
Below: Possibly the most northerly route of the Irish Sea is the Ballycastle-Campbeltown service operated by Sea Containers. The *Claymore* is pictured here at Ballycastle during her first season on the newly-established route. *(Matthew Punter)*